George Morrison
An Irish Camera

Pan Original Pan Books

List of Illustrations

To Theodora who has helped me throughout and been my constant and creative critic

Acknowledgements

The visual material for this book has been brought together from many different sources, and I particularly wish to express my thanks to Dr Richard Hayes, at the time of my research Director of the National Library of Ireland, and to his successor in that office, Dr Henchy – both of whom have, over many years, given me every possible encouragement and assistance. I am very much indebted also to the kindness of Dr D. Thomas and Mr J. Ward of the Science Museum, South Kensington, for access to a number of early calotypes.

My grateful appreciation is also due to Ms Rosemary Atherton, at that time keeper of photographs in the Magee Institute of Continuing Education of the New University of Ulster, for her helpfulness in enabling me to establish the period of the photographs of Londonderry.

The Old Dublin Society has likewise been of very great help to me in making available many excellent photographs of Dublin and its environs in the 1890s; and my thanks must also be given in this regard to the librarian of the Dublin Civic Museum for her kind assistance.

First published 1979 by Pan Books Ltd,
Cavaye Place, London SW10 9PG
© George Morrison 1979
ISBN 0 330 25640 8
Filmset by Crawley Composition Ltd
Printed in Great Britain by
Butler & Tanner Ltd, Frome, Somerset

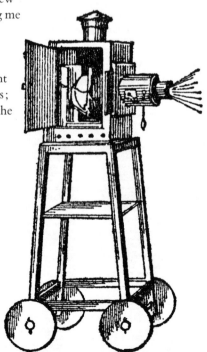

Introduction

It was in France that photography was born. In 1826 Joseph Nicéphore Niepce, a lithographer and inventor, after an exposure of eight hours produced the world's first permanent photograph: a dim and fuzzy impression of his farmyard. He later joined forces with a Parisian scenery designer, Louis Jacques Mandé Daguerre, who gave his name to daguerreotypes, which had exposure times of about half an hour. These, the first practical photographs, were launched in 1839.

An English country squire, William Henry Fox Talbot, advanced the camera towards today's portable machine with the discovery that lenses of short focal length were much faster. He was thus able to replace the large camera obscura, which he, like Daguerre, had been using with a small camera. The key to speed was the concentration of dim light on a small piece of emulsion, using lenses of short focal length. Fox Talbot's small box camera with sophisticated improvements was what most people were using almost a century later.

Country Life and the Land

As this collection and others show, the camera came to Ireland early in its history. In 1850 an Irish contemporary of Fox Talbot's, John Shaw-Smith, was the first person to photograph the ancient city of Petra – 'the rose-red city half as old as time'. A significant contribution to the development of photography was made by another Irishman, Thomas Grubb, a lens-maker who was born in Kilkenny in 1800. By 1840 he was making telescopes, and in 1860 built the largest telescope in the Southern Hemisphere for Melbourne, Australia. A lens made by Grubb in the mid 1850s is in the London Science Museum. His son Sir Howard Grubb made telescopes for the Government during the First World War and the place where he had his works in Dublin is still called Observatory Lane.

Also in Dublin at the beginning of this century, Professor Joly of Trinity College was working on colour photography and established a company to sell do-it-yourself kits for colour photographic positives.

Because of the exposure time necessary, until the 1890s a photograph could not be taken as instantaneously as photographs today. It was nonetheless a radical break with the portraits which earlier generations had taken for granted. No longer could the qualities which society admired be imposed on the sitters in the same way as the portrait painters of the eighteenth and early nineteenth centuries had done. Painters like Gainsborough always managed to infuse their family groups with goodness and virtue. Likewise in France, Boucher and Fragonard portrayed a universal sweetness. The early camera could record a well-organized composition but it could not show virtues or emotions which were not in the faces of the sitters.

The earliest scene in this collection is of a Cork Street in 1845. The picture has the posed correctness of a stage set and misses the gossiping groups, the sympathy with suffering of the later studies. It is in the ordered tradition of Malton and Bartlett, whose engravings had captured the Ireland of earlier generations. Here is the timelessness of painting or drawing rather than the instantaneousness which the camera would bring us.

We have grown accustomed to the honest realism of the camera; the bullet-riddled assassin's victim on the front page or the television announcer's warning that 'this film is explicit and may cause distress'. But the effect of these on our hardened sensibilities must be mild compared with the impact of a photograph of an eviction to the Victorians. The smell of poverty, the blank incomprehension, the inheritance of resentment are all there. The camera had taken its place as an instrument for social reform. For the first time, photography showed the underprivileged as they really were. No longer would the poor appear in the way that Hogarth had depicted them, as subjects for sermonizing, or examples of depravity.

The changes which the nineteenth century brought to Ireland were not paralleled in the rest of what was then the United Kingdom. The Act of Union launched the new century with a complete change of emphasis for the country. It put an end to that confidence which had grown up in the last quarter of the eighteenth century, the outward and visible sign of which had been the building boom throughout the land. Stately mansions, square, solid farmhouses, merchants' homes, town houses for the landed gentry, schools, great public buildings and churches, all sprang up in an elegant style which has never been matched in Ireland, before or since. There had still been, of course, tensions in society but it had looked as if the Irish were going to sort them out themselves. As everywhere else in Europe, it had still been the era of the privileged, but their affluence had at least given employment – some crumbs had fallen from the masters' tables. The Union stopped this development with the suddenness of a revolution. Building ceased; Dublin, which had been the second city in the Empire, degenerated to a provincial capital; and the resentment which was to grow as the century progressed began to be felt. At this time Britain was learning to live with the effects of the Industrial Revolution, a development which only touched the north-east of Ireland. The only photographs of heavy industry in this collection come from the shipyards of Belfast.

Because the Victorian age was a period of economic stagnation there, Ireland has few great nineteenth-century buildings. Among the photographs the only significant one is the Salthill Hotel in Monkstown, County Dublin. Large family hotels like this were built at the popular resorts as the sea-side holiday became a feature of life for those who could afford it, as in the rest of Europe. Another exception to the lull in construction was the building of churches, usually Gothic, after Catholic Emancipation in 1829.

In the 1840s the general picture of Ireland was one of poverty and misery for the great majority of the people. The eviction photographs bring home the wretchedness of the conditions which the poor had to leave for even more uncertain futures. In the census of 1841, houses were graded into four categories, the lowest of which consisted of windowless mud cabins of a single room. Nearly half the families of the rural population lived in houses of the lowest category. The pathetic furniture was considered as luxury. In 1837 in one townland in Donegal the population of 9,000 could boast only of ten beds, 93 chairs, and 243 stools between them.

Potatoes were easy to grow and had become the basic item of diet. Thus when the crop failed in the mid-forties, a famine of appalling proportions spread across the land; in the short space of five years more than a million had died and 800,000 had sailed for the New World. The population in 1841 had reached over eight million; now, almost 140 years later, it is only about 4½ million.

Because the population was so drastically reduced by the Great Famine, a rapid change in the average size of farm resulted. During the remainder of the century the trend towards larger farms continued. However, only a small proportion of the population actually owned land, and this was to lie behind political and other action for many years. In 1870, before the first Land Act was passed, only 3 per cent of the population of the country owned land. Forty-six years later the figure had grown to 64 per cent. This radical change had been brought about by a number of far-seeing measures implemented by successive British governments.

The Great Exhibition of 1853 must have been to famished Ireland what the Festival of Britain in 1951 was to war-scarred England. Guide books were published, visitors came and tourism, which has ever since been one of the most significant contributers to Irish revenue, was established. The extending railway network carried travellers all over the island. The Salthill Hotel (see **37**) charged visitors to the Exhibition 3/- for a bed, 2/- for breakfast and 3/- for dinner, whereas more modest establishments like Jurys in Dublin charged 1/6, 1/9 and 2/- respectively.

The organization of efficient public transport was to have far-reaching effects not only for the people of Ireland but also for those who came to visit. Bianconi Mail Cars were introduced in 1815 and the newly-built railways opened up a countryside hitherto unknown to travellers who were already familiar with the beauty spots of the mainland of Europe. One of the early visitors' guides, *A Tour in Ireland A.D. 1806* by Sir Richard Colt Hoare, reflects this sense of a voyage of discovery to an unknown island, felt by tourists before the organization of efficient public transport:

'To the traveller, who, fond of novelty and information seeks out those regions which may either afford reflection for his mind, or employment for his pencil, and especially to him who may be induced to visit the neglected shores of HIBERNIA, the following pages are dedicated . . .

'While the opposite coats of WALES and SCOTLAND, have for many successive years attracted the notice and admiration of the man of taste, and of the artist; whilst the press has so teemed with publications, pointing out their natural beauties and works of military and monastick art, that little more is left to be described; whilst WALES and SCOTLAND, I say, have had the assistance of the Historian's pen to record their annals and of the Artist's pen to portray their natural and artificial curiosities; the Island of HIBERNIA still remains unvisited and unknown. And why? Because from the want of books and living information, we have been led to suppose its country rude, its inhabitants savage, its paths dangerous. "Were we to take a view (says an Irish Historian) of the wretched condition in which the History of IRELAND stands, it would not be a matter of astonishment that we should be considered as people, in a manner unknown to the world, except what little knowledge of us is communicated by merchants, sea-faring men and a few travellers, while all other nations of Europe have their historians to inform their own people as well as foreigners, what they were, and what they are".'

Reading on, we discover that one of the reasons why the enquiring tourist should discover Ireland is because:

'We can no longer in safety ascend the steps of the CAPITOL, nor wander peacefully along the luxuriant shores of BAIAE or MISENUM; even the frozen regions of MONT BLANC are interdicted to us by the ferocious decrees of a CORSICAN DESPOT.'

Napoleon's unpopularity may have been one reason and no doubt there were others, to cause the visitors to begin visiting Ireland. Later in the century the camera no doubt also played a part in introducing the beauty of the Irish countryside to people all over the world.

Tourists were unlikely to be encouraged by

photographs of industrial activity, but the shots of the Harland and Wolff Shipyard in Belfast (see **26, 27**) are among the most interesting social records in this collection. There was no obvious reason why this industry should grow up in Ireland, as almost all the raw materials had to be imported and there was no ready home market for the finished product. It grew, nurtured by Sir Edward Harland, a man with engineering skill and business ability; his partner G. W. Wolff being less prominent in policy making. But from an early age Harland interested himself more in local and national politics than in his company's affairs, and they had both retired from the shipyard by 1892. Nevertheless they had chosen a worthy successor in William James Pirrie, who became a partner in 1874 and was to become a pioneer at a period when the growth of international trade and passenger travel was becoming significant. The 10,000-ton *Teutonic* of 1889 was followed ten years later by the 17,000-ton *Oceanic*, and in 1911 by the doomed *Titanic*, four and a half times as large. When Pirrie entered into partnership with Harland and Wolff there were 3,000 employees; by the outbreak of the First World War there were 12,000. Pirrie followed his former partners into the world of politics and was Lord Mayor of Belfast in 1896; in 1897 he began the building of the City Hall.

Pirrie's political stance as a Liberal won little support in a country which at the time was becoming politically polarized, and his greatest contribution must be as the most important industrialist in the country of his day and the world's greatest shipbuilder.

Now, although living conditions have improved enormously for the majority of people in a century and a quarter, it is noteworthy how little public buildings and places have altered from the time these photographs were taken. The Library of Trinity College, except for the closing of the arcading on the ground floor, looked very much as in the photograph in this collection (see **2**) right up to 1978 when the new Fellows Square was opened. Stately homes survive, even though more people share in their glories than a century ago. The railway stations which remain do not look all that different, and many of the smaller roads of Ireland are much as they were when brave cyclists risked life and limb, more than three generations ago.

Harold Clarke, Dublin

Preface

Why does the past always look more alive in photographs than in paintings?

Very little has been written on the subject of the unique quality which characterizes the actuality photograph as a source of communication with, and as an aid to, the understanding of the past. It is a simplex system in which the past is always sending, the present receiving, both more or less effectively. The word 'actuality', as a concrete noun, has only come into use relatively recently, being promoted by the French use of the word 'actualité' to mean a film of an event which has not been artificially staged for dramatic purposes.

What is it that the photograph gives us that is not found in the work of even the greatest painters? It is something approaching a direct look at the past through eyes that are at the service of a twentieth-century mentality.

The fundamental importance of this special circumstance is apparent when one considers the way in which recent work has shown the visual world to be perceived. Dr Richard Gregory, the Director of the Brain and Perception Laboratory of the University of Bristol has given, in his two fascinating books, *Eye and Brain* and *The Intelligent Eye*, a vividly illustrated account of how our visual perception of the world is dependent upon our internal 'object hypotheses'.

All drawn and painted documents, all sculptures are the products of artists' conceptions, and thus strongly influenced – both consciously and unconsciously – by their attitude to life, which is a function of their cultures. Photography is historically the earliest system whereby visual information can be, in part at least, recorded *without passing through these selective processes*.

Naturally, a photograph too is closely circumscribed by cultural and technical curtailments produced by its period; but, unlike a painting (though this may have in it some information of which the artist was not consciously aware at the time of painting) the photograph, particularly the nineteenth-century photograph, records a great deal of information that the photographer was not in the least concerned with, either consciously or unconsciously. Much of this content may have been so commonplace to the photographer that it would have been altogether excluded from his attention. Photographic records preserve many such details which, today, are often of greater interest than the ostensible subject consciously recorded; thus the future may look more directly at the past.

The highly specific techniques of late twentieth-century photography, while they give greater scope for its development as an art, can actually diminish its richness as an informational source for future observers. A specialized use of photography and holography, designed to capture and preserve the maximum of simple information, might well be developed as a contribution to the needs and interests of posterity. Although isolated instances of work of this kind can be found almost from the earliest days of photography, no great body of co-ordinated work on an international scale has been undertaken to provide the future with better photographic records of what will shortly become the past.

λόγos* has been a magic word in European culture over so many centuries. The very recent developments of non-verbal communication systems finds institutionalized learning still rather unawakened to the rich sources of information that exist *outside* the symbolic language of words – archaeologists and art-historians, naturally, being excepted. The bewilderment of some academic historians when confronted with non-verbal sources of information is still a prevalent feature of this decade, as was shown during the seminar on 'Film and the Historian' held a few years ago at London University. More encouraging is the general public's growing acceptance of non-verbal sources, as shown by the ever-increasing demand for books and films of a visual-activity nature.

The earliest photographs of Ireland that survive date from just before the Famine. There are, however, no photographs expressive of the suffering incurred in that great social disaster.

There are two chief reasons for the absence of any Famine photographs. Firstly, the speed of photographic emulsions was at this time so slow that only posed photographs could be taken, thus making candid camera techniques impossible; and secondly, there were, in the Famine years, very few photographers working, in a few of the principal towns, and these were almost exclusively occupied with studio portraiture. In fact, with a few very rare exceptions, of which the photograph of William Smith O'Brien (see **6**) and the beautiful calotypes by Fox Talbot (see **3**, **5**) furnish examples, photography in Ireland hardly emerged from the studio until Scott-Archer's wet-collodion process was well established.

The demand for stereoscopic photographs, for use in the ever increasing number of stereoscopes to be found in Victorian drawing rooms, led to the establishment of the Irish Stereoscopic Company, which, for the first time, undertook nationwide photographic work. Later, the greater convenience of dry plates had the effect, in Ireland as elsewhere, of further increasing the number of photographers working in the field – as distinct from the studio. Consequently, from the late 1870s onwards a greater wealth of material becomes available.

The earliest Irish examples of candid camera techniques are to be found in the work of A. V. Henry and Dr Garratt in the 1890s. Quite a few Irish photographs of the '90s and early 1900s have appeared in recent publications. For this reason I have concentrated mainly on the periods up to 1890 and have used the lesser known but exceedingly interesting work of Henry and Garratt to exemplify the period 1890–1910.

As this book is not intended to be a history of photography in Ireland, but rather a window opened onto the past, I have felt myself at liberty often to select detail from the photographic material to illustrate aspects of the life of the times, rather than, in every case, to present all of the photographs in their original cadre. Let us then open that window onto a world which is so greatly different from the one in which we live.

George Morrison, 'Atlanta', Dalkey, Dublin, 1978

* *Logos* – knowledge, The Word.

Cathedral, Marlborough Street, Dublin, 1845

Ireland
in the 1840s

1 A street in Cork, 1845

In 1845, six years only had elapsed since the French Government made a gift of the daguerreotype process to the world, in which period photographers using the process had established themselves in many European cities. From one such daguerreotypist comes what is probably the oldest surviving photograph of an Irish scene in existence, taken by John Mott.

The exposure of some five to ten minutes has not enabled any of the people in the street to be clearly caught; but the blurred shadow of a child sitting on the edge of the kerb and one or two faint figures in doorways can just be made out. The houses, built by the rich merchants of the late 18th century (a time when Ireland had a parliament of her own and had a measure of control over her trade) are now, in their commencing dilapidation, showing signs of the decay of industry which was one consequence of the Act of Union of 1801.

This and the following eight photographs give us a glimpse of Ireland just before it was struck by one of the greatest peace-time social disasters to be experienced by a European country since the Middle Ages – the Irish Famine.

2 The Library, Trinity College, Dublin, 1845

This delightful building, which for dignity, grace and functional design can compare favourably with a product of any age, was built in 1712 from the designs of the architect Thomas Burg.

In this photograph, which is the earliest in existence of the building, blinds have been lowered behind the windows to protect the books from the light, the angle of which suggests late afternoon on a late spring day. The two figures in caps, knee-breeches and gaiters are college porters in their livery; the other figures appear to be students.

4 Dublin Castle, 1845

Soldiers of the Guard on parade in the Upper Castle Yard. The figure of Mars, by Van Nost, above the gateway on the right, no longer has his spear, which gives him, today, the air of making a rhetorical declamation.

Since the coming into operation of the Act of Union in 1801 and the Rising of 1803, a large British army had been kept in Ireland, garrisoned in the principal towns and supported by the force instituted by Sir Robert Peel, the paramilitary Royal Irish Constabulary. Dublin Castle was the centre of British administration in Ireland.

The original Castle of Dublin appears to have been built around the earlier half of the 13th century, but successive rebuildings and repairs have quite obliterated its original structure. It contains some elegant and charming interiors by Francis Johnston.

3 The Front or Parliament Square, Trinity College, Dublin, 1845

This Fox Talbot calotype shows the Front Square viewed from the position at which the Campanile was later built, and one notices too the absence of the clock in the pediment of the Regent House on the right.

The steps of the Examination Hall on the right seem to have been as popular a sitting-place then as they are today. The college porters still retain their characteristic livery with their huntsmen's caps, but the dress of the students has changed vastly! The carriage is a typical 'inside car' of the period.

5 A family group in Hardwicke Street, Dublin, 1845

This detail from a calotype of 1845, by Fox Talbot, clearly illustrates the necessity of remaining still while the exposure of several minutes was being made. Those at the right who have moved hardly appear at all. The minute hand of the clock in the tower is blurred over a compass of around four minutes, which shows us very exactly how long the exposure was.

An interesting feature of the clothes of middle-class people at the time was the comparatively poor fit to be observed in nearly all photographs of the period. A certain bagginess about the trousers and ill-fitting jackets and coats make a striking contrast with the dress of people in a similar income group today.

6 William Smith O'Brien and Thomas Francis Meagher, 1848

Thomas Francis Meagher and William Smith O'Brien were leaders of the rising of 1848 which was Ireland's contribution to the 'year of revolutions'. At the time of this photograph they had had sentence of death passed upon them, but the following day this was commuted to transportation. The figure on the right with the key is the gaoler. The extreme demand for copies of this genuine photograph led to its being faked with actors, and some copies of the spurious photograph still survive.

Fair Day, 1910

Country
Life and the
Land

7 A Kerry Spailpín, *c*.1868

'Spailpín' is the Gaelic word, Anglicized as 'spalpeen', to describe a landless wandering labourer whose only capital was his health and strength and perhaps, as it may be for the individual in the photograph, his spade. The disastrous agricultural and economic policies of the first half of the 19th century in Ireland produced such men in enormous numbers. They had no training which would encourage their employment in industries abroad, where unskilled work was still being undertaken by women and girls; and when work became increasingly unobtainable in Ireland they were obliged to emigrate whenever they could find the money to do so.

Such men became famous for their labour as navvys on the rapidly growing canals and railway lines in England, Canada and the United States. They have left behind them a rich tradition of folk-music, among which is one of the most beautiful songs in the Gaelic language – 'Cuainín Spailpín'.

8 An old woman at a 'Holy Well' *c.*1865

Thousands of these wells are to be found throughout Ireland, and although most now have a legend attached to them pertaining to an early Christian saint, their sanctity goes back far beyond Christian times – as the ancient folk-tales of Ireland bear witness. Springs have been sacred to all ancient peoples.

The broken bottle on the right is for the convenience of visitors who may wish to partake of the waters. Nowadays an old china cup is usually found in its place.

9 A traditional fiddler, *c.*1870

The photograph has rather a posed air about
it, reminiscent of the many pictures of Welsh
ladies in steeple hats playing the harp in very
stilted poses – and like them it was probably
made to supply the demand of tourists.

Nonetheless, it is by a good few years the
earliest photograph of a traditional fiddler
that survives.

10 Collecting slops for feeding pigs, 1870

These boys are collecting ends of uneaten food of all kinds, vegetable parings, potato peelings and stale bread, which has been reserved in the houses on their round in a receptacle called the 'pig bucket', one of which is seen in the photograph.

These buckets were emptied into the barrel which, in the course of a day, acquired an aroma of a character not to be put into words. This mixture was then boiled up and, either with or without further additions, was fed to the pigs which were often kept in styes off the back lanes of both the larger and smaller towns, contributing to the locality a smell now rarely experienced.

11 The battering-ram being brought into action during an eviction, Vandaleur Estate, County Donegal, late 1880s

While soldiers stand by, the Sheriff's officers set up a tripod from which to suspend the large battering-ram which is to be seen at the right of the photograph.

A particularly interesting detail is the intricate network of rope on the roof of the cottage, so much more elaborate than the simple cross-ropes seen in picture **13**. These intricate patterns of the straw rope, called 'sugán' in Irish, and the associated stone keys for anchoring the rope (seen projecting at intervals from the top of the wall) were absolutely essential if the thatch was to be prevented from being torn away by the Atlantic gales which are such a prevailing feature of the West of Ireland.

12 Huts improvised by the Land League
to house evicted tenants, early 1880s

After an eviction (see **11**) the family, especially
if they had contributed to the Land League
funds, might be rehoused by the League in
improvised dwellings such as these, one of
which is obviously a caravan. Roofing-felt of
the period is to be seen on the top of both
structures.

The large round pot in the foreground is the
traditional Irish three-legged pot, a vessel
differing little in general shape from the
cauldrons of the Bronze Age, though made of
iron and having short legs.

13 An evicted family, County Donegal,
early 1880s

The father, mother and three children have
been evicted with their very meagre
possessions; battens have been fastened across
the doorway to make the act of re-entry a
matter of 'breaking and entering'.

When eviction occurred to a family the
possibilities before them were rehousing by
the Land League in improvised huts (see **12**),
emigration (see **7**), or building a 'sod cabin' on
the nearest available land, in which they were
often helped by neighbours.

This particular family chose the latter, as can
be seen in the next photograph.

14 A 'sod cabin' built by an evicted family in County Donegal, early 1880s

The same family as seen in **13**. The sod cabin was built by selecting an area of vacant ground and digging out an area equivalent to the inside of the cabin to a depth of two or three feet so that the compacted subsoil was reached.

The spoil from this excavation was used to form an earthen bank around the edge with the exception of the area of the intended doorway. Next, a wall of turf sods; grass-side down, was built on top of the earthen bank sloping up to a point at the centre of both ends of the house. Straight branches of trees or other timbers were then laid across from end to end; and, finally, a series of long overlapping strips of turf, grass downwards and supported on timbers, was laid to form a roof. Generally, a hole (in this case near the end wall on the right) was made to allow smoke from the fire on a hearth-stone to pass out. The builder of this cabin has managed to incorporate a small glass window to admit a little light into what must have been a very dismal habitation.

15 An elderly smallholder
after eviction, 1880s

Clifton Castle, County Galway

Country Houses

16 Gate Lodge of Dromana House
and bridge over the Finisk river,
County Waterford, *c.* 1870

This very charming and original gate lodge
to the Dromana demesne was built by the
Villiers–Stuarts around 1840, in a style
reminiscent of that of the Royal Pavilion,
Brighton. It is one of the very few buildings
of this kind, in an uncorrupted form, to be
found in Ireland. It had become much
dilapidated in the course of years and when,
after the recent sale and partial demolition of
Dromana House, it was in the greatest
danger of being lost, the Irish Georgian
Society undertook its restoration which was
accomplished with complete success.

17 The Fort, Hillsborough, County Down, *c.*1868

This part of the Fort, Hillsborough, was built in the 1650s by Arthur Hill, the ancestor of Arthur Wills Blundell Sandys Roden 5th Marquis of Downshire, seen seated in the foreground with his huntsman and gamekeeper.

The three windows between the towers would have been enlarged to the form seen in the photograph about a century before it was taken, at the same time that the doorway was altered to the form in which it appears. Very interestingly, one half of the original iron-bound doorway is to be seen leaning against the base of the tower at the left. Such houses, in their original fortified form, were typical of the kind of dwellings that the Scottish planters of the 17th century, granted the lands of the dispossessed Irish, were obliged to live in – to secure themselves against the raids of the still unsubdued original inhabitants: a social legacy of ideological and religious separatism difficult to accommodate even in the 'civilized' 20th century!

18 Members of the Vaughan family in front of
their house, Buncrana Castle, County
Donegal, early 1870s

The house was built *c.* 1817 by Sir John
Vaughan, from materials forming the bawn
of nearby O'Doherty Castle in which they
had previously been living. Even a century
ago, as the photograph shows, signs of
dilapidation were present, and this has
continued up to recent years – the more
unfortunate as the house is a pleasing example
from a period from which few houses survive
in Ireland today.

19 The gatekeeper's daughter, Randelstown, County Antrim, c.1860

The 19th-century gateway is that of Shane's Castle and is now all that remains of the Victorian house (destroyed by fire in 1922) which was built near to the ruins of two earlier castles, belonging to the O'Neills of Clandeboye, the first of which was destroyed in 1490.

The baron's coronet above the gateway indicates that the photograph was taken later than 1855 when, on the death of the last Viscount O'Neill, the Reverend William Chichester, the heir-general, assumed the name of O'Neill by Royal Warrant, and was created Baron O'Neill of the United Kingdom.

20 Carton, Maynooth, County Kildare,
c.1870

Although the FitzGerald family have
associations with the region of Maynooth
going back to the end of the 12th century, it
was not until shortly before the middle of the
18th century that Robert FitzGerald, 19th Earl
of Kildare, bought the property of Carton
from a cadet branch of the Talbots of
Malahide. Richard Castle was engaged to
rebuild the house in 1739, but the 19th Earl
died the year before this was completed in
1745.

His son later became the first Duke of
Leinster, and the property remained in that
family until after the Second World War,
when it was bought by Lord Brockett. The
property has now been sold.

21 Luggala House, County Wicklow, *c.*1870

Luggala is one of the most romantically situated houses in Ireland, placed a little back from the sandy shore of a mountain lake, the sides of which rise steeply from the water; in one place the bare cliff has, from a certain angle, the profile of a giant face. Behind the house are steep slopes covered in woods. Edward Odell of Carriglea in County Waterford gives this description of visiting there in September 1830, when the house was in the possession of the La Touche family: 'Sunday, September the fifth. We walked to church at Delgany and after that departed for Luggela (sic) in a jaunting-car. The wind had been very high all day, but on turning the corner where you first come in sight of the lake and house, there was such a blast that it was almost impossible to walk against it. Monday, September the sixth. We were to have left Luggela early but it was so wet that we waited until half past nine for the rain to moderate. We went the short way over the mountains and we were obliged to have a bullock to help draw the car up the hill, besides some men to keep it steady.' From the La Touche family, the estate passed to the Guinness family. A few years ago a fire severely damaged the house but it has been completely and conscientiously restored.

Derry shirt factory, *c.* 1904

Industry

22 Baltimore Maritime School,
County Cork, *c*.1890

Around 1880, the Baroness Burdett-Coutts
was influenced by the extreme poverty in the
vicinity of Baltimore in West Cork – an area
that had never recovered from the devastation
of the Famine of 1846-1849. She deposited a
fund of five thousand pounds in a local bank
from which the parish priest could draw to
provide local fishermen with 50 per cent of the
money they needed to buy a fishing boat; the
boat builders agreeing to take the remaining
50 per cent in instalments from the fishermen.

This scheme was so successful that the
Government, with assistance from charitable
trusts and very generous help from the
Baroness herself, set up a school to train boys
to be fishermen. This school was opened by
Baroness Burdett-Coutts in 1897 and over the
years provided the basic training for boys
from all over Ireland, most of whom became
seamen.

The photograph shows a net-making class
in progress.

23 The stripping room, Goodbody's
Cigarette Manufactory, Dublin, *c*.1890

In a modern cigarette factory, machinery
carries out every process from the moment the
tobacco arrives until the packing cases of
cigarettes leave the factory. Only eighty years
ago this was all performed by hand. Here the
girls are stripping the soft parts of the tobacco
leaf from the ribs. This gives us a good idea of
how in a 19th-century 'manufactory', where
everything was carried out by hand, work
could be just as monotonous and boring as on
a 20th-century assembly line.

One notices too that none of the girls have
any support for their backs! Light is supplied
from a skylight and an arc lamp. Such arc
lights were the form that electric industrial
lighting first took in Ireland.

24 Men and boys working in Smiths
Hosiery Factory, Balbriggan,
County Dublin, 1890

What we today would call child labour
continued right up to and into the 20th
century; these boys cannot be more than
about fourteen years of age. The boy on the
right is loading an hydraulic press, which will
probably be operated when full by the
foreman on the left. Gas lighting is used in
this factory, as electric light for industry was
not yet available outside the cities of Dublin,
Belfast and Cork.

25 Sewing 'Balbriggans', 1890s

These girls are employed by Smiths of
Balbriggan to do finishing work on the
woollen stockings that have for generations
been known and worn by Irish people both at
home and abroad. The term 'balbriggans'
originated in the United States. Curiously
enough, woollen stockings have become
fashionable again.

26 Using a hydraulic riveter during the
construction of the SS *Oceanic*, Harland and
Wolff's, Belfast, early 1890s

To control this huge and cumberous piece of
machinery four men were needed. Three are
seen in the photograph and a fourth is
operating the crane. Nowadays this is done
with a pneumatic riveter which can be
carried by one man.

The 1890s and early 1900s were the great
periods of ship-building in Belfast, when
some of the world's most outstanding ocean
liners were built there. See also **27**.

27 Building the SS *Oceanic*, Belfast, 1898

This White Star trans-Atlantic liner was launched in 1899 from Harland and Wolff's shipyard in Belfast and represents one of the most famous achievements of that yard which has had such a significant part in the history of big ship construction. She had a gross tonnage of 21,274 and could make 21.5 knots with compound engines of 29,000 horsepower. The pride of the Belfast shipyard workers in their work can be seen in the way they have assembled to be photographed.

28 Making china, Beleek,
County Fermanagh, 1892

A discovery of a suitable felspar in Beleek led
to the establishment of a pottery there which
has been famous for over a century for its own
very distinctive form of glazed Parian ware.
The local felspar has been exhausted for some
years, but the pottery continues to be made
today with felspar imported from Norway.
A particular feature of Beleek ware is the
porcelain basketwork which is achieved by
building up a network of thin rods of still
moist china-clay, made by extrusion, upon a
former, until the delicate open-work bowl or
dish is completed; then very intricate flowers
are applied petal by petal. The whole is then
allowed to dry before the first firing.

29 The Export Department,
Jacob's Biscuit Factory, Dublin, *c.* 1890

Together with distilling and brewing,
Jacob's biscuit factory was one of Dublin's
chief industries, also established in the
eighteenth century. By the 1890s it had
already penetrated markets in the far corners
of the world, as can be seen from the
addresses on the packing-cases. Jacob's
were pioneers in the use of electric lighting in
Ireland, taking their supply from the Dublin
Electric Light Company as early as 1882.

30 The Maypole Dairy's Ice-plant,
Dublin, 1892

In the days before small refrigerators, this
progressive firm installed an ice-plant to
supply its chain of dairy shops throughout the
city with ice to keep its dairy produce fresh.
Special insulated containers had not yet been
developed and the ice was packed into barrels
either as large blocks or else crushed in the
machine at the left. In hot weather the barrels
were surrounded and covered with straw so
that, on the slow journey to their destinations
by cart, the ice would have a better chance of
arriving unmelted.

Railway bridge over the Boyne at Drogheda, *c.* 1866

Communications
and Ports

31 The Old Tollbridge, Ferrycarrig,
Wexford, late 1850s

Transport in Ireland during the 19th century
had to depend on many wooden trestle
bridges such as this, similar in almost every
fundamental respect to the type of bridge that
Julius Caesar built across the Rhine. The toll-
house and gates are seen at the far side and on
this side is seen a pile of planking which was
needed for the constant repairing of the
carriage-way. The rattling, rumbling sound
produced as the iron-tyred wheels of carriages
passed over the planking was a frequent cause
of dismay to ladies who felt that at any
moment the bridge would give way and
desired their coachmen to 'go slow so as not to
have us in the river'.

32 Ferry Point, Youghal, 1868

Ferry Point is in County Waterford and
Youghal, where Sir Walter Raleigh lived and
where he first cultivated the sweet potato – in
County Cork – for the noble river Blackwater
is the boundary of the two counties. To get
around by road, via the old Youghal bridge,
would have been a distance of nearly seven
miles, whereas the distance across the narrow
neck of the sheltered estuary is barely a
quarter of a mile: a perfect site for a ferry. The
motor-car has brought about its demise.

33 George's Quay with the Custom House, Dublin, *c.*1860

James Gandon's magnificent Custom House creates an unforgettable atmosphere of civic dignity and civilized charm as one looks across the Liffey from George's Quay. Note, however, the primitive handling techniques for unloading from the colliers that are alongside the quay.

34 Shipquay Street, Derry, *c*.1865

Derry has been a port of commercial importance since Viking times and, like all old ports situated on hills, it has many streets running down to the river – a feature of all towns built by the Norsemen.

Shipquay Street shows the delightful character that the city possesses of charming, dignified 18th-century and early 19th-century buildings; the vista at the top of the hill is closed by the Corporation House.

The street passes in the foreground through the original walls famous for withstanding the siege of 1689.

35 Public conveyances in Patrick Street, Cork, late 1860s

In the twenty or more years from the time when the Fox Talbot photograph (**3**) was taken, there had been hardly any change in the form of vehicles for public hire. To us today, accustomed to a much more rapid rate of change, perhaps only the Volkswagen 'beetle' can be given as an example of a vehicle which has remained the same in appearance for so long. In this photograph, taken by the

Stereoscopic Company of Ireland, one can clearly see the characteristics of these vehicles which up to the late 1870s provided the usual form of private transport in Ireland.

Though Irish roads were good for their day, the extreme variability of road surface and gradient demanded a favourable power-to-weight ratio in the design of vehicles that were to fulfil their function economically, hence the light construction: the single horse had to pull the minimum weight that was not pay-load!

The wet weather disadvantages of the outside car, the nearest to the foreground, are very apparent but it can be seen that the inside car, next in line, while it gave a measure of

protection from the rain, mud and wind, was much more cramped and gave little opportunity to the tourist to admire the scenery! For this reason, the 'jingle', as these vehicles were called, was generally much less popular than the 'side-car', though often resorted to in wet weather. It was an Irish form of 'one of those hackney-cabriolets which have the door behind and shoot their fares out, like sacks of coal, upon the pavement' – as Charles Dickens described it. The less favourable power-to-weight ratio of the four-wheeled Brougham restricted its use in Ireland, as indeed elsewhere, until roads had sufficiently improved to render it practicable when pulled by a single horse. The 'inside car' existed in a more elaborate form in Dublin where it had glazed rear windows and a door.

36 North Quay, Drogheda, *c*.1870

Drogheda had considerable industry as a centre of linen-making, iron founding and brewing. Much of the port traffic was still sail in the 1870s, the ships in the photograph being mainly colliers.

It is interesting to note that the vessels are berthed at a distance from the quay wall to avoid being stranded on mud at low tide; and the mode of access is a very narrow plank for a gangway, with sometimes a hand rope beside it.

In the background is the Boyne railway viaduct, built for the Dublin and Belfast Junction Railway Company by Sir John McNeill, and appearing in its original lattice girder form, now replaced by a more modern construction which makes use of the original stone piers.

37 Conversation on the way to the train, Monkstown and Seapoint Station, County Dublin, *c*.1870

This, the first railway to be built and to provide a public service in Ireland, was established by Act of Parliament in 1831, construction beginning in the spring of 1833. Running from Westland Row in Dublin to Kingstown, now Dunlaoghaire, it was opened to the public on 17 December 1834 – barely five years after the opening of the Stockton and Darlington Railway in England.

The original track was the 4ft 8½in standard English gauge but, after the line had been taken over from the original company by the Dublin and Wicklow Railway, the gauge was, in 1857, increased to the standard Irish gauge of 5ft 3in, which is seen in the photograph and remains the Irish standard to this day, giving extra roominess to Irish rolling-stock.

In the background is the Salthill Hotel of which Thackeray gives an account in his *Irish Sketch Book* of 1844, but which was destroyed by fire in 1973:

'Not far from Kingstown is a house devoted to the purpose of festivity: it is called Salt Hill, stands upon a rising ground, commanding a fine view of the bay and railroad and is kept by persons bearing the celebrated name of Lovegrove. It is, in fact, a sea–Greenwich, and though there are no marine whitebait, other fishes are to be had in plenty, and especially the famous Bray trout, which does not ill deserve its reputation.'

The advertisement for a concert publicizes the inclusive ticket issued by the railway company – combining return fares with admission to the concerts on Kingstown pier, a popular evening excursion for Dubliners.

38 Waiting for the horses: a Bianconi mail car outside the Clifden Bianconi Car Office, Clifden, County Galway, early 1880s

The last of the Bianconi services to operate ran between the railhead of the Midland Great Western Railways in Galway and Clifden, a town on the west coast fifty miles away. It remained in existence until the mid 1880s, being replaced by a light railway which, in its turn, has given way to the 20th-century motor-bus.

'A Bianconi mail car is nearly three times the size of an ordinary side car, and when on a dark night it advances, Cyclops-like, with but one eye, it is difficult for even a sober driver to calculate its bulk.' – extract from 'Lisheen Races Second Hand', a short story from Somerville and Ross's *Some Reminiscences of an Irish RM*.

39 'The Scrap-Iron Express', Terenure,
County Dublin, 1910

The Dublin and Blessington Steam Tramway
passed through many vicissitudes during its
existence of some forty-four years. It
commenced operations in 1888 and came
finally to a stop on 31 December 1932.
Running along by the side of an ordinary
road, without any fencing between its
permanent way and the road itself, it is hardly
surprising that there were many casualties; a
good number of them fatal. The memorial
crosses erected on the site of these fatalities are
said to have prompted a tourist to enquire:
'Are people often killed?' To this he is said to
have received the answer: 'No, generally only
once!'

The locomotive seen in the photograph was
purchased by the company in 1906 and
remained in use until the closure.

40 Curragh at Kilkee, County Clare, 1872

Curraghs are a kind of boat developed from
a very ancient model. A waterproof
covering – which in early times used to be the
tanned skins of animals, but for more than
two hundred years has been tarred calico –
is stretched over a light wooden framework.
Although appearing very flimsy, the boats
are astonishingly seaworthy and ride over the
waves with the lightness of a floating gull.

The variety of curragh developed in Kerry is
probably the most graceful, but that which is
built on the Clare and Connemara coasts
and on the Aran Islands and which is seen in
the photograph is the kind with which people
abroad are most familiar from Robert
Flaherty's film *Man of Aran*.

41 Catching the ferry, Glandore, *c.* 1885

The highly indented coastline of parts of
Ireland, and the wideness of some of the
drowned estuaries, meant that – before the
advent of the motor-car – a great many ferry
boats were in use. The countrywomen in the
photograph are about five or six years behind
the times in their fashions, which in remote
parts of Ireland at that period was quite usual.

42 Castle Street, Dalkey, County Dublin, 1898

Electric trams began to replace the horse trams in Dublin in the last years of the 19th century. Here is one of the early Dalkey electric trams near the terminus in Castle Street. An interesting detail is the complete absence of any advertisements on the vehicle, which has only just come into service.

The tram has come to a stop at the very end of the tram lines. The conductor is standing beside it and the driver is inside. At first the tramways in Dublin were operated by different companies, who would not allow the vehicles of another company to run over their own tracks. Because of this the Dalkey line originally only ran as far into town as Landsdowne Road; but in 1904 the separate companies were merged in the Dublin United Tramways Company which operated them all and established a through service from Dalkey to Nelson Pillar, which became the centre of the tramway network.

44 On the way to Valentia Island, *c.*1868

Valentia Island, which is on the extreme south-western end of Kerry, was the site of the cable station where the first successful trans-Atlantic telegraph cables entered the ocean. In the photograph the telegraph line is the one connecting the Atlantic submarine cable to Dublin and to London via Portpatrick.

The photograph is taken a few miles from Valentia and it is strange to think that messages from London and New York are passing these figures who are making their way by side car along the road. Telegraphic communication between Valentia and Trinity Bay, Newfoundland had first been achieved in 1857, but the first cable was ruined in an attempt by an engineer to use too high a current and voltage. Although, with difficulty, messages were got through it for a little over two months, the cable had been so severely damaged that it then failed completely. The second cable opened communications in September 1866 and proved much more successful – although it only operated until 1877. By that time there were four more cables in operation including one from France. The slender thread in the photograph was one of the first great communications advances.

45 The harbour, Carlingford, *c.*1865

The little town of Carlingford, in County
Louth, at the head of Carlingford Lough, was
a place of importance in the Middle Ages as
can be seen from the ruins of the castle
commenced by Hugh de Lacy in the 12th
century and subsequently extended.

King John is said to have passed three nights
here. In the foreground are to be seen a tripod,
scales and weights for weighing the catches of
the fishing boats which are alongside the pier.
After being bought by dealers at the ports it
was loaded upon specially built light carts
which set out at top speed to carry it into the
heart of the country for resale while it was
still fresh.

Ennistymon, County Clare, 1880s

Tourism, Sport
and Leisure

46 Punchestown Racecourse, *c*.1856

From the opposite side to the grandstand, one
notices the great contrast between the rich and
poor. A wagonette has an elaborate meal set
out, while beneath it poor women beg for
scraps of food. In the centre of the photograph
the roulette woman has set up her table but, at
the moment, the crowd is much too interested
in what is going on on the course for her to do
much business.

47 A guide waiting for tourists, Dinish Island, Killarney, *c.*1858

Judging by his clothes and his clay pipe he is probably one of the guides who waited at various points to show the sights of Killarney to tourists.

The short clay pipe, like the 'churchwarden', has almost completely gone out of use – though members of the 'Pipe Club' at Keen's English Chop House in New York could until last year still have the delectable experience of calling for their clay after dinner, and enjoying a unique combination of two great smoking pleasures: a churchwarden filled with one of the most delicious pipe tobaccos it has ever been my experience to encounter.

Before using a clay pipe the mouth-piece should always be covered with a layer of sealing-wax as this prevents the pipe from sticking to the lips.

48 Dubliners on an outing to the Scalp by side car, *c.*1865

The Scalp, at about eleven miles from Dublin where the main road to Enniskerry passes between two steep hills, has remained popular and unspoiled to this day as a place for those living in the city to get away from bricks and mortar. It takes its name from the distant appearance of the rounded hill covered with young pine-trees presenting the appearance of a closely cropped head of hair.

The young trees, which have just begun to establish themselves on the hillside to the left, now form an impressive dark wood which greatly adds to the atmosphere of the place. This rear view of an outside car very well illustrates how the passengers were accommodated with their legs outside the wheels, their feet resting on the foot-boards of the 'wings'.

The soft, unmetalled character of the road surface on what was an important thoroughfare is also of interest. The mud which forms itself into ruts would, in dry windy weather, become clouds of dust. The traveller would arrive at the end of a journey covered from head to foot in grey powder.

49 A middle-class couple at Glendalough, County Wicklow, *c.* 1865

One has only to look briefly at these two figures to realize the extent to which the dress revolutions of the last seventy years have freed us from the tyranny of clothes.

Imagine going for a ramble in the country surrounded by yards and yards of cloth and hoops; or having to take with you a tall silk hat which, on your return, would require half an hour or more with a special brush, before it could be safely put back into its case! Should the day have proved wet, the anxiety and annoyance caused by the fear that the singular symbol of respectability might perhaps have suffered irreparable damage must often have been the occasion of much domestic tension!

The lady's heavily oiled hair shows that the Victorian 'antimacassar' was no frivolity but a severely practical necessity.

50 Bunratty Castle, County Clare, *c*.1875

Although more intact than the great majority
of Irish castles, this late 15th-century seat of
the O'Briens of Thomond was in a very
advanced state of dilapidation when the
photograph was taken just a century ago.
Nevertheless, it is interesting that it was
considered to be a tourist attraction then. The
amount of careful restoration work on the
exterior of the fabric carried out by Viscount
Gort after his purchase of the castle in the
1950s was matched by an equal amount of
work on the interior, which was furnished
with an interesting collection of late-
medieval furniture and objets d'art.
Entertainments in 'medieval banquet' style
are now given there nightly.

51 The guide shows the 'Deer Stone' to a visitor to Glendalough, County Wicklow, *c*.1870

Glendalough, in County Wicklow, has been a tourist attraction since the 18th century, both because of its many antiquities and for the great beauty of its scenery. In the background, to the left, is the round tower, seen here before its top was restored with the original stones by the Board of Works in the mid 1870s.
Next to it is the 9th-century St Kevin's Church with its belfry, an unusual feature in early Irish churches; while beyond it to the right are the remains of the cathedral dating from the 10th century, with 12th-century additions.

The stone in the foreground, to which the guide is pointing, is a 'bullaun' or stone quern for grinding corn. Many of them are to be found at early monastic sites in Ireland – and they have frequently, in later times, been used as fonts. A tradition has gathered around this particular one that Saint Kevin, the late 6th- and early 7th-century hermit, near the site of whose cell the later monastic city of Glendalough grew, milked a deer into the artificial hollow of the granite stone at a time when he had no other source of milk.

52 At the 'Twin Wells' source, Lisdoonvarna, County Clare, *c.*1875

The 'Twin Wells', Lisdoonvarna, has remained to this day a popular Irish spa, although the primitive arrangements made for the visitors who came to take the waters still continue in much the same style. The waters of this source contained sulphur and iron. Three large glasses are seen, obviously for the use of those who wish to benefit by the medicinal waters of the springs; and a small glass, standing beside a 'black bottle', suggests that the custodian of the well can also supply 'strong waters' of indeterminate origin to those who, for medical reasons of course, might wish to benefit by them. This last convenience is now to be had only at the licensed premises in the adjoining village and only 'proprietary brands' are now available.

53 Bathing boxes and a donkey for hire,
Kilkee, County Clare, late 1870s

Kilkee has been a popular Irish resort for sea
bathing since the 18th century, but the
elaborate 'bathing machines' seen on English
beaches of the period are here replaced by the
modest bathing-box which continued in use in
parts of Ireland up to the 1930s.

The donkey is shod while the donkey-woman
goes barefoot! The lady in the straw hat
appears flattered to be included in the
photograph.

54 Regatta in Kingstown (now Dun Laoghaire) Harbour, 1883

The magnificent harbour at Dun Laoghaire, constructed by the famous engineer Rennie, has always been a favourite place for holding competitions for all the smaller sailing boats; and this kind of regatta is still held today.

55 Setting out for a spin on a 'penny-farthing', Dublin, 1890

Although rapid advances in the development of the bicycle had rendered obsolete the penny-farthing type, there were in the 1890s quite a few veterans of an older generation who regarded the chain-bicycle as an effete and degenerate vehicle. Some of these continued to ride the alarming looking, older machines up to an advanced age; but after the 1890s the ranks thinned, and the coming of the motor-car rendered this form of the sport too perilous.

Photograph by A. V. Henry.

56 'Bloomers' in full bloom, 1890

These ungainly garments, probably the most ungraceful apparel ever invented for either sex, were very much in evidence in the late years of the last and the early years of this century. The scene, which is the long straight avenue in the Phoenix Park, and the suggestion of intentness in the body-mechanic of the figure, give one the impression that the lady is practising her cycling. Such fantastic garments illustrate very well how in either men's or women's liberation it is the internal inhibitions that need to be overcome – after which the external trappings vanish of their own accord!

57 The Generation Gap, County Dublin, 1896

This smart and very up-to-date lady cyclist has just pushed her modern machine with its pneumatic tyres to the top of the long hill at Kilternan, and is obviously on her way for a pleasant spin down Glencullen and home through the Pine Forest.

On her way she has fallen into conversation with the elderly countrywoman who seems both amused and fascinated by her young companion. The subject well illustrates the photographer A. V. Henry's advanced approach to what we would call today the candid camera snapshot (see also **55, 59**). This style was beginning to come in during the 1890s and early 1900s, as witness the work of Count Giuseppe Primoli in Italy and Jacques Henri Lartigue in France. It is pleasant to observe that in Henry we had a practitioner of the style in Ireland before the turn of the century.

58 A Dublin
cycling club,
County Wicklow,
c.1890

Mud pies, Dolphin's Barn, Dublin, 1900

Dublin
Diversions

59 A meeting on the way to the Strawberry
Beds, County Dublin, *c.*1890

These southward-facing slopes near
Castleknock, County Dublin, were known
for the excellent fruit which their sunny
aspect, rich soil and good drainage provided.
A walk or ride to the Strawberry Beds was a
frequent excursion for Dubliners in the
summertime.

Photograph by A. V. Henry.

60 Afternoon tea in Glenageary,
County Dublin, 1898

The paraphernalia of the late-Victorian tea
party are well exemplified in this photograph:
the hot-water kettle, kept simmering on its
spirit stove, and the 'slop-basin' into which
was poured away the dregs of the previous cup
(to the left of the tea-tray nearest to the
camera). The piano stool on which the
gentleman on the right is sitting hints that
there may have been music to follow.

61 A smoke in the coach-house, 1899

Throughout the whole of the 19th century
and even well into the 20th century,
particularly in Ireland, smoking in the home
was only considered permissible in smoking-
rooms, suitable out-buildings – as in this
photograph – or in the garden, if ladies were
not present. When young men assembled
together for this purpose it was known as
'raising a cloud' or 'playing Jupiter'. (Jupiter,
who wielded the thunderbolt, was accustomed
to 'raising clouds'.)

62 Dancing bear, Glenageary,
County Dublin, early 1900s

Until as late as 1914 these itinerant bear-
keepers were to be seen in Ireland, though few
had as fine an animal as is to be seen in this
photograph.

After the First World War, motor traffic had
become too dense for this kind of street
entertainment to be possible, and people's
attitudes to the treatment of animals had also
begun to change.

Officers in Court dress, Dublin Castle, 1900

The End
and the Beginning

63 Members of the Irish Volunteers
(the Home Rule and, later, Republican force)
drilling near Dublin, 1914

This force, together with the Irish Citizen
Army, formed the nucleus of the Irish
Republican Army after the Easter Rising
of 1916.

The suspension of the Home Rule Act in 1914,
on the same day that it was passed, inevitably
led to significant changes in the Irish political
scene being brought about by
unparliamentary means.

64 F. E. Smith, later Lord Birkenhead, addressing a loyalist political meeting near Belfast, 1914
Sometimes history repeats itself in a singular manner. A prominent Tory politician of the day addresses an anti-Home-Rule rally in a manner strikingly resembling that of Mr Enoch Powell in Northern Ireland today.